About the Author

He's a lovely man. He lives in Devon now. He's done a lot of things, like keep bees, design buildings and landscapes for sacred use, build the buildings too, have kids, lecture in fine art, watch birds endlessly, farm a smallholding, live in Osho's communes and in cities and in desert places on several continents, teach art as therapy, make furniture, write articles for international magazines, do nothing in a cave, exhibit his paintings, grow organic vegetables, have lots of grandchildren, write a book and get really into beekeeping.

These poems are the work of the last two years, the drawings of the last thirty.

Life is one Blessed thing after another, Rashid's first book of poems and drawings, is also published by Tree Tongue and is available from the web site.

This book and others available at
www.treetongue.co.uk

rashid maxwell

Published by Tree Tongue
2 Chapel Downs Cottages,
Crediton, Devon. EX17 3PB
www.treetongue.co.uk

ISBN 0-9546099-7-2

Offering

poems paintings - all the arts -
are trying to say what can't be said
they are failures from the very start
yet i think of them as prints left in the sand
grasses bent or signs and scrapings
left by one who's passed this way

i lay out in the open these faint traces
of the passage of a heart
with love and thanks
to beloved nisheetha
to my amazing children
their exquisite children
to osho
and the lovers friends and travellers
with whom i share this pathless path
you too nishok

Contents

Who we Are

On this brilliant daffodil morning
the corporate directors
sit comfortably about the boardroom table
the chairman wants to know
what's going on
wants a business plan for filling all the vacant lots -
wants shopping malls industrial estates
many-tiered sports and leisure complexes

This of course is metaphor for ego
ego too abhors the vacant spaces
ravishes resources to arrive
at pro tem satisfaction

On this brilliant birdsong morning
the fluting thrush winds
through the greening woods
an email tells us of a good friend's death
we feel his radiant energy within us
strong and clear as ever
he never was his body
just a minor shareholder in it

What is revealed in vacant spaces
say both the ancients
and the quantum physicists is
life
that fire won't burn
that water won't drown
that a sword won't kill
nor earth overwhelm

Let trees and boggy hollows flourish
undermine the tower blocks of belief -
or else where will
who we are
find place
to be?

The Real Cost

the real cost of a poem
is how many thousand journeys
to hear a single echo?

can we pay in trampled blades of grass
or raindrops on the deeps of time?
the forms are variously magnificent

halls and sumptuous state-rooms
bedrooms probably uncountable
set in grounds as varied as the earth can show

open to the public all and every day
our memory is the winking lights
a christmas tree appears and disappears

i have to smile - though not at memories
the hugeness of existence pulls my mouth apart
ah now you have the measure of my drift

excuse me i must leave again
beloved the real cost of a poem
is everything - pay gladly

Sing your Life to the Bees

Rain fills the landscape
Fills the heart with tenderness
The bees are settled for the winter
Sing your life to the bees.
They know.

We are pilgrims on a journey with no destination.
We are a rational species with no reasons for our being.
We are hunters of a fragile prey that vanishes when sought.
We have five senses and we can't perceive the all-pervading presence

We are diamonds believing that we're pebbles.
We are attar of bergamot pretending to be twice-warmed tea.
We are prospectors in a desert trying to find sand.
We are in free fall looking for direction.

The doctor says the cure is never certain.
He hands me the prescription - one
enigma well digested three times daily after meals.
He presses the red button;
as the floor gives way he says, 'Wait . . .'

Rain fills the landscape
Fills the heart with tenderness
The bees are settled for the winter
Sing your life to the bees beloveds.
They know.

Waiting Naked in the Field

thistles docks and nettles
overgrow me

waiting naked in the field
she doesn't show up for our dates

i have been celibate so long
it feels like promiscuity

my penis now no more nor less important
than my Adam's apple or a kneecap

she cannot be contacted
with words of any kind

i'm waiting for a different mating
a penetration that is inconceivable

*

after weeks of bedrock drought - rain falls
moth wings on dry grass

I wake up in her arms
the dawn glow fills our room

we have always been here
always been enfolded

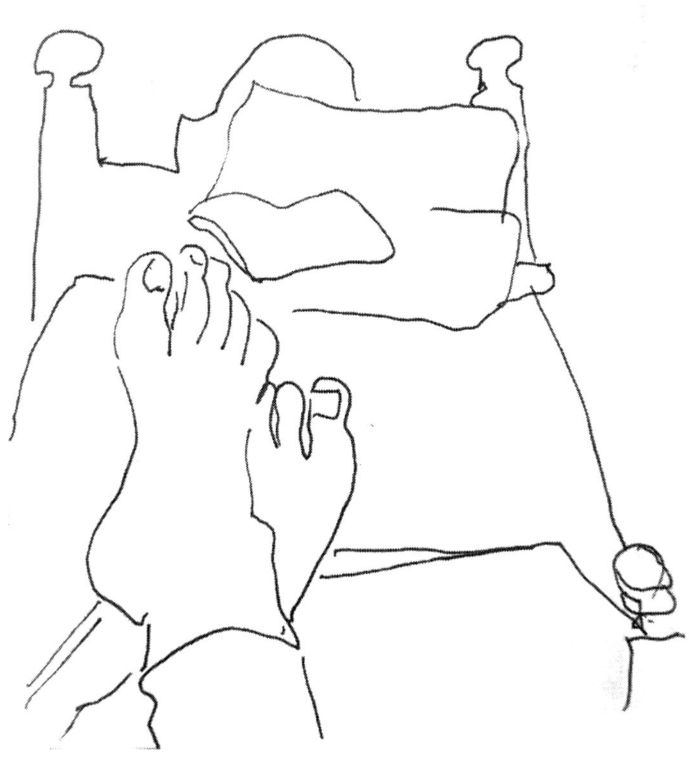

Sand Dunes at Braunton

(" . . . one of the last really wild habitats left in the UK."
UNESCO Biosphere)

the dunes welcome spring
with orchids and thistles
a windfall of waders and warblers
pale cobalt skies
and a thousand weekend tourists

spring is a current of life essence
my word for unity or consciousness
of a fineness so fine
to the mind imperceptible

binoculars around my neck
grandsons bouncing footballs off
the curved sand-screes
we move in the
infinite field of fineness

from a high point we aim
for the brilliant blue barrier
over the slacks
over the ochre strip of mobile sands
white waves disperse into spray
its easy enough to glide

mind blunders forever between
pleasure and pain
a tilting world war gun emplacement
engulfed in rapture

now the boys tiff and bicker
creating each their separate minds
i stand on the wild shore yelling
the current - mind the current
let the current sweep you away

Voice from Afar

Poets should in no way concern themselves with human relationships - but should get to the very bottom. Francis Ponge

I dread the silence of the telephone
this hazy summer day of blackbird's song
of dog roses and foxgloves in the barricaded hedgerows
of villages slow drowning in the heaving tide of brambles
always waiting for the call

waiting in the violet shadow of an oak outside the hospital
I try to understand, try to understand
there is violence in my sadness as well as in her awe-ful act
I turn my eyes away from what the mirror holds
turn a deaf ear to the squabbling of seagulls
the mobile is a millstone on my hip
a deadweight on my heart

she carves her own trail through this vale of pain
regardless of my pointing out the scenic wonders
regardless of my hopes to make good on my fatherhood
I confuse attachment with compassion
feel the lamprey sucking on my hip

tonight
the full moon
is reflected
in the darkness of the Bristol Channel and
the dark corrupted waters of the Avonmouth Canal
yet it remains
untarnished
silver in the night sky
pure reflection of a burning star.

the silent telephone will shrill
life has to happen as it will

Remember?

remember the pinpoint in the void?
remember?

how
that pinpoint of infinite density
sneezed?
a big bang
how
the gasses fled cooling slowing changing form
crusting into galaxies nebulae constellations asteroids planets
meteoroids red giants quasars pulsars white dwarfs comets suns the
wandering moon?
how
the soup of minerals and chemicals
made bacteria and dinosaurs and my dad
who smarmed his way
into my mum's brittle knickers?
another sneeze
and trouble began

they called me you naughty boy
this and that
disobedient disgraceful a disappointment
so when
aged fourteen
i fell out of a
giant cedar tree
and my whole life flashed before me
i knew
i knew it wasn't like that

ideas and ideals multiply like wild comb
in a beehive filling up the void

jackdaws clatter on the slate roofs
people of Iraq scatter in the fields of fire
everything was in that pinpoint universe

sometimes when the car stops
in the wilderness of silence
in the ticking of the cooling motor

then i
almost
remember

He Wants to Know

He wants to know the time
I don't know what time is

He wants a hot shower
I am a warm cascade

He wants to read a gossip magazine
I see only coloured dots on white

He wants to clear out the top shed today
I say it is clear already - always has been

He wants to go for an afternoon walk
I ask where on earth can he go?

He wants to write a poem
I feed him drops of honeydew

He wants to make love to his woman
I am everlasting orgasm

He would like to know who he is
I am

He says for god's sake stop this divisive dialogue
I say - Quite.

28:01:05
HERCU

Looking for Meaning

looking for meaning in the numbers in
our bank account and on our voice mail

I wonder
if we'll we ever find wisdom
I wonder
what we are
why we are
who we are

looking for meaning in the numbers of
our children and the speakers at our funeral

I wonder
at the purple rain clouds laid across
the eager ochre hills we only notice
when the car breaks down
and plans crumble like
old mud from the chassis

looking for meaning in the numbers of
our prized possessions and subordinates at work

I wonder
at the writer's art
torn flags
planted in trust
over tumbledown ramparts
in the depths of unknown territory

looking for meaning in the numbers on
our birth chart and our circle of acquaintances

I wonder
at passing beauties
admiring not desiring
the smell of warm earth
after summer rain
engulfing us

what are we
why are we
who are we

most wonderful is
that we are!

Good bye Disha

dark clouds slide across the hill
in the last rays of summer sun

all afternoon we hauled
and cut and stacked the winter logs

checked each beehive for its winter stores
the memory of Disha rises brilliant

in the dusk - vital like a star
last Friday she left her pregnant body

she grew up in the commune with my kids
she was the child of all of us

circled around the world said someone
sannyasins turn our PC's into a cyber

Buddha Hall Osho is in silence
rain and sunlight flood our hearts

love is the air we breathe honouring her
who was a light unto herself

chill air settles on the valley floor
the moon is full tonight

it's only words that say she's died
won't we all know soon enough what that means?

What People Here Adore

What cannot be thought with the mind, but that whereby the mind can think; know that alone to be Brahman, the Spirit, - and not what people here adore. Upanishads.

in the great undiscovered cave
there's no chance of sleep
the dance goes on
till all hours

drop down the secret shaft now
now while the music pulses
while we're on the subject
join the perennial celebration

the upstairs neighbours bicker
flash adorable thighs recreational vehicles
audible visible mp3's
they trample to collapse the roof

outside the night wind
rushes like a hungry fox
you see that which can not be seen
when you become invisible

now the cave
is bigger than the world
includes the Dow Jones holding firm
while Man United slide into the Bardo

sit up properly
spirit brings the gift of nothing

You are so Unreasonable

you're so unreasonable
just because I look at that girl in the street
it doesn't mean I want to sleep with her
this is not the first time that you've erred

jumping to conclusions
I only have to say one word to her
and you call it chatting her up
trying to get off with her

okay so we have a goodbye hug
you call her look blatant come-hither
no need to sling dirt she's not a flirt
it doesn't mean a thing

and even if I do meet up with her
so what? you project your fears a lot
on nothing
on just how a thing appears

it doesn't mean I want to be with her
just relax and try to understand a simple fact
just because I sleep with her
it doesn't mean that I don't

love you even though
you're so unreasonable

The Zigzag of Our Lives

whoever lives this body
hands out accidents and blessings

accidents are blessings
allies on our search
for what we'll never find
because ha ha
we are it
whether
kicking balls against the tall wall of the building
lobbing jokes into the crowded amphitheatre
fitting bookshelves in the alcove

it isn't quite so black and white
this zigzag of our lives
the ball the wall
the people in the terraces
are creatures of our
little minds

yet
sitting silently not thinking - feeling
not feeling - being
in the surface drift of floating leaves and bubbles
trees and sky reflected on the dark furred bones
of riverbeds

we are ourselves creations
reflections
in the cosmic mind of No-mind

Take to the Air

take to the air with me
keep rising in love
fifteen second affairs that come to nothing

the sound of rain on the window frame
the patient standing of trees in the wood
and of pine boards on the floor
a woman running to her lover in an orange grove
the rug reflecting starlight from nights in the frosty desert

look beloved
the dull crimson glow of the stove
one log settles into another
we stare at the mottled intimacy
of ash and flame

beloved ones who meet on this page
let's leap before we look
pass together through the white flower
whose veined wings and tongue of fire lift us
out of gravity

we thought god was just the beauty of the morning in the forest
and of the evening sky above the high street
a beautiful woman watching from an upstairs window

its you too isn't it

Black

Hauling long poles on my shoulder, stowing them on a truck, a passer by called out "It's the end you can't see you have to watch."

forget about the television deities
annihilation of the five old villains
of the senses
happens in the black hole of the night
go joyfully towards the dying of the light

the window frame blinks gold
against the blue-black sky
the leaves of the beech trees heave
gloss black matt black
enter with a bow
the massive gateway of the dark

this big black hole is scary
it is a cleaning situation
black is the new white

with the villains unemployed
then we can't avoid
the long home that we once enjoyed
the everlasting ever-present void

for with nothing to relate to
the relater vanishes too
in that immense treasury of emptiness
insensible
stay! stay there when already
blackbirds sing to the pale colours of the summer morning sky

it's the end you can't see you have to watch

A Nobody

brown mist drifts from the sky as rain
the days are dark and drawing in
our lanes run slick with sadness
i want to commit despair

at boarding school I had a cops n' robbers
game of cards called I Commit
no one ever played it with me
i first encountered despair

that hunchback imp called
imperfection lives on behind my stylish
house my humpty dumb profession
my blaring shop front smile

until the lights go down
old age gapes now
my days lack driving force
up pops the knobbly imp

how is it to be without a mission? asks the imp how is it to be useless? how is it to be a nobody?

wait till i tell you
come out
with me into
the brown afternoon

rain drifts upwards from the folded valley
where the alders edge the stream
above my head arch
branches of a hedgerow oak
droplets cling to every leaf and mossy bough
the leaves are autumn red and gold and green
this nobody has never seen a tree
so present so alive so beautiful

$n(a+z)=0$

Show: n(a+z)=0

where *a* is summer blue
on swallow's backs
blackberries guddled from the brambles
love flowering after lunch bodies laughing lustrous as dolphins
the smell of woodland resting
our improvised creations begetting their own jubilation

and *z* is monday morning
fighter planes appear in my name from low glaucous clouds
to decimate your village
leaves of autumn stagger into restless congregations
the forecast for the week drab
the only highlight root-canal work friday 5.15

a plus *z*
times n for any mix and quantity of
good and bad
pain and pleasure
e.g. witnessing how many raindrops tapping secret letters in a hidden library plus hibernating suction-wrapped in fear and toothache

the mystery
requires both
then only is there balance
0
zero shunyo the void

oak trees grow their noble height
as much from storms as sunlight

therefore *n(a+z)=0* QED

The Question of my Self

Who,
Who am I
Talking to, running from, nucleating round?
Who am I in love with?
Who sorts the red and white
Petals of love?
Whose scent do I catch through the boarded-up door?

In whose presence do I,
Sleepwalker, shame myself? Whose sword echoes
In the ruined palace?
Who excites me with brilliant desire?
For whom was this cartwheel
Of rough-spoke words composed?
Who?

Whose attention do I barely mention?
For whom will I lie down
In white lilies?
Who is glimpsed in strange places,
By night,
Immense, deserted, blind, anonymous? Who prods
My fears?

Whose shadow follows me by night
When I stumble imperiously home?
For whom shall I keep a place vacant at table?
Who am I trying to kid?
Who shoots me down,
Loots my slim identity?
Who arranges this strange account of my life?

gold ochre
gold ochre

Last Night

late last night
installing headphones
on my
new laptop

i somehow opened up
a porn site sad slag women
sucking whopping

dicks of shadow muscle men
of course i was appalled
and fascinated

watched three sixty second clips
went downstairs trembling
sat beside the dying fire

while battered mouths
and thrashing greasy members
overrode my thoughts

these greyhound hormones
lie waiting at their starting gate
i want to invite

all frantic guys
to stand with me
naked

in the silver rain
amongst the autumn oaks
feeling

the never ending
orgasm
of nature

My Girlfriend Left

This afternoon my girlfriend left
left me floating in a void
outside the window
ropes of rain
beat down the sodden heaps of leaves

I've lit the oak logs in the stove
my surrogate TV
flames flit and mutter and
I too flit in and out of time

In time is misery unworthiness
old age and loneliness
out of time is wordlessness
spaciousness and ease of being

Even when the fire dies down
the dark night fills
with warmth and light
and what my girlfriend is

To be Divine is Ordinary

to be divine is ordinary
putting your feet up in the living room
when everyone's in bed
heaven is that silent place
we travel to and from

so many things can be explained
and still remain mysterious
i only have to touch
the vacuum cleaner with my toe
and it will gobble up
invisible dust motes
from rugs of intricate
vibrating loveliness
made in some unknown
spacious time
in war torn turkmenistan

when the phone rings
i hear of a son rising
from a grandchild's womb
while the white winter sun
sets punctually at 4.23
tell me how are these
extreme eventings realised?
and choreographed?

to be divine is ordinary
the old man on the mountain says
we do not have to be
especially intelligent or gifted
we already are godlike
and about god
a word so totally discredited
charred and bloodstained
don't worry

just recollect the gift of trust
creates an attitude of gratitude
from time to time put up your feet
in the quiet house of the heart

A Different Melbourne

for Kavisha

I have in mind a Melbourne of the mind
Where streets are broad and traffic-free
Where Nature is both temperate and kind
None suffer from anxiety

With you I visited a kindred place
You opened up a thousand doors
We moved into a brilliant sparkling space
The air was full of lovingness

Your songs are water in a droughty time
Patterns of an inner sky
Sunlight on the peaks we long to climb
Ancient magic minstrelsy

Beloved one there is no barrier
Between two old beloved friends
I send this little verse to be a carrier
Of a gratitude that never ends

I dedicate to you this work of art
Creator of a Melbourne of the Heart

2nd August 07

Vision from Afar

One granddaughter spends all day
awash in
the effluence of television watching

I tell her that in my eyes
our human eyes are made exclusively
for looking at reflected light
different depths and hues and tones
not direct light

I cross the room and open up the window
the scents of new mown grass and roses drift into the house
the scents remind me of the joyous times when I was farming and
we hauled the bales of hay up into the barn with pitchforks and a
horse and cart and drank a keg of elderflower champagne

I tell her furthermore that in my eyes
television has made the world's cultures into sterile deserts
corroded communities
created human robots

I know she says
but it makes me laugh

HOTEL
CRYSTAL

Beyond Belief

"Well what do you believe then?"

The farmer's wife threw down the question
with the carrots beetroot and potatoes.

"What I believe is actually beyond belief.
May I ask - do you believe that you exist?
Or do you know it?"
"I exist alright. I know it To believe is to know as they say"
"I disagree," I said. "To believe is not to know. We weave ourselves a banner of allegiance.
On one side is belief. On the other side - doubt.
Most of the mayhem in our warring world comes from this clash of banners.
For me, it makes more sense to stay
Floating in the inland sea of not knowing."

"I believe that when I die I'll go to heaven.
That's four pounds fifty please."

I can see, from where I sit, Mahavira, unmoving for a thousand years

Going on Sixty-Eight

(Consciousness is all there is: the Purpose and the Source.)

Next month he will be sixty eight.
He thinks he's only eight.
Where are the missing sixty years?
Has it got too late?

They were a movie on the telly
He saw but didn't watch,
Relieving all the usual fears
With a modest tot of scotch.

He saw himself a cardboard artist
A father rather too uncouth
A good companion to his peers
And a seeker after truth.

Now the truth emerges
From his self-improvement course;
Beyond the laughter and the tears
He always was the Source

A Passing Notion has its Say

old disciples wait for their inheritance
they hear the church bells pealing
in another country

we've raised the sacred airy buildings
we've struggled with the pigments to create skies
we've scattered words to germinate abundance
and how would you describe our
tearing down the glory of
the rainforests?

we've passed on our genetic torches
we've loved and been abandoned
we've lusted and despaired and been inspired
and how would you describe our
piling up of stone and glass into a
vast cathedral?

we've gathered in the pumpkins from our gardens
we've set by cords of fire-wood for the winter
we've worshipped to the muslin sound of bees
and how would you describe our
plundering the carbon from this
precious earth?

we've dropped our youthful helpfulness
we've seen the secret signals of the master
we've heard the silence in the market place
and how would you describe the
focussed rage of we who put
mankind in space?

do not take it personally
you waiting old disciples
no need to fidget or grow fretful
what if we are only passing notions
in the revels of the
wiped out gods?

08 12 06
08 10:12

A Poem for Jordan

I
I am
I am that
I am that I
I am that I am

I am that I am I
am that I am I am
that I am I am that
I am I am that I
am I am that I am
I am that I am I

am that I am I
am that I am
I am that
I am
I

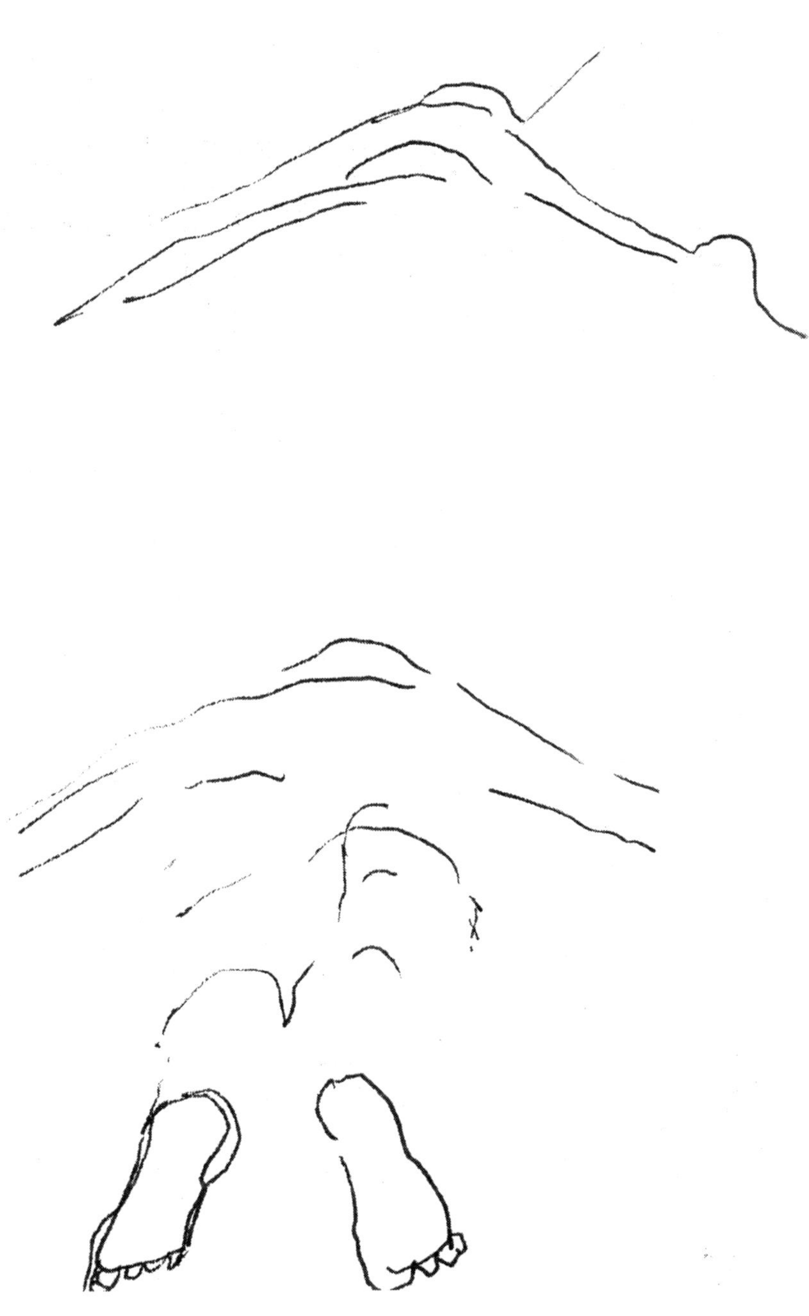

Including Death

"The Sufi teaching is that love is god"

call me narcissistic and deluded but
I do not want
the dark hole of the future at my feet
the endless bloody conflict
with success and failure
the fear of not being who I think I am
I do not want
to fall
but to rise in love

you are narcissistic and deluded

call me optimistic and a dreamer
I want
to launch above this world
of misery and doubt
of fuck-ups and the fear of death
of all varieties of limits
into realms of
freedom spaciousness
contentment

dream on

love is a great bird of power
she will bear me up

oh please!
what do you mean by love?
the momentary relief
of your ego being massaged
or what they call
the great breaking down of boundaries
your ego totally annihilated
the river flowing into the ocean

yes the love
that spreads through
everything
including death

it's your life friend!

Eloi Eloi Lama Sabachtani

What to say if you are being nailed to two crossed pieces of wood

Do you mind?
Hey! Leave it out
Give me a break

Please!
Please!

Okay.
If that's how it is
I give up.

Don't worry!
I won't even
Hold it against you.

You have to do
What you have to do
And that's perfect.

Thanks!
Thanks!

A Little Birth

for Michael Z

bright cerulean blue
clear winter sun behind

the woods rush through my eyes
these written words through yours

as will the world rush through the cloudless eyes
of your welcome newborn daughter

home birth or caesarean section
goodness or its absence

bright sun or drumming rain
the years rush through

little princess snappy blonde super-chick,
menopausal grandmother sick old-age

and again
the bright cerulean blue

who is the one who is born
and dies?

don't try to answer

Queen of the Night

the invitation comes
at any time.
night or day.

urgently i climb
the turret's
hollowed stair.

silk hangings, gold candles,
persian rugs,
flute, tamboor, drums,

looped garlands, fragrance
of the small white florets,
queen of the night.

for a time - sometimes -
we talk of mundane things
joke about the mysteries,

wander in each other's eyes,
speak of love,
above all

of love that weaves
electrons and neutrinos
into place.

you hold me to you
past and future slip
your brocade robe too

we are one
we are
one

Today I am the Rain

today I am the rain
yesterday we lay behind a dune
submerged in winter sun
in the ocean's stillness

the entrance way was through a tiny
portal in the high blue wall of sea
stars shone throughout the day
in the ocean's stillness

the gateway vanished
a passing surfer said
it might come on another
wave - another time

today the one who rains outside
stares down appearances -
putting out the garbage
is the void moving on the void

sand drifts down upon itself
Kali dances on the chest of Shiva
we're all living upside down
eating pasta with a cleaver

Breasts

women
lovers friends and wives
in the street or of the street
my mother
shopkeepers nurses teachers models
you've nourished

and enlivened me
with love and lust
the milk of human trust and kindness
also and above all with the
softness of a summer hayloft that dispels
awhile the hardness of this life

the pressing need for sex
for all that huffing and exertion
faded
i still love
immersion in breasts
the soft

softness of them
emblem
of a generous nation
that briefly mitigates
obliterates
this hard hard life

as a school kid i had dancing lessons with a ballerina she held me so
my eyes made contact with her pointy breasts that didn't damage me
the softness made me hard later courting i learned the knack of
flipping up the hooks of bras in the back seats of my best friend's car
far-out transport

often i have laid my head
between a pair of breasts

laid liquid in that woman's love
slid into the small death of ecstasy

when big death comes
i won't protest
i will be proud to be your guest lay
my head between your breasts

Perfection

Leonardo wanting to impress a Prince,
Drew a perfect circle on the whitewashed wall.
An ancient Greek artist depicted grapes in bunches
So lifelike that the birds flew down and tried to eat them.
My friend, enfeebled with MS, lives in a home
For old ex-servicemen who can no longer stand
Up straight or shine their boots and buttons every day.
Please don't give us all that shit about perfection.
Let us be flawed and hum-drum as we are.

At school I tried to be like Chapman in the sixth.
Everybody told us we were never good enough.
Then we tried to be like Bradman or Matisse.
It never crossed our minds that we were okay as we were.
We started out the journey feeling guilty and inadequate;
Either we became depressed or busted ass to get ahead,
And now we cross the border into uselessness.

Then its twenty four hour television and
A tumbler full of pills, waiting for the bitter end.
This is not a plea for tolerance or even
Better funding for the ageing and the dying,

I am recommending hard core imperfection;
Butterfly-flitting, woman-loving, heartfelt,
Guitar-strumming, flower-smelling, dolphin-hugging,
Late-night dancing, colour-daubing, time-wasting imperfection.

Samasati

For Puja

There is one love she said and i could
see what she was pointing to
a kookaburra dropping on a lizard
below the terrace at the edge of paradise

we are dreaming in a land of broken dreams
time washes down the rocks nothing ever finishes
or starts - lizard into bird, bird turns into dingo
dingo into humus and humus into tree -

that's the love she's pointing to
samasati means awareness of the sparkles in
the polished air the ringing of the unseen crickets
one love - endlessly recurrent

not - she'll be right - but
she *is* right - no worries

I am the Earth with my Legs Apart

he sits in my study the long curtains drawn
our poet
tonight he's the passionate rain
giving all he's got
vigorous and tender implacable
all of him
sizzles with naked desire

i am the earth with my legs apart
watching his passion stir my flowers
inciting exciting
he penetrates now
my deepest parts
i will love this rain forever

we are the source overflowing
we are the audible silence
we are lost in the ecstasy

his energy pours
he waits with his violent seeds
when he bursts
he keeps coming
keeps coming keeps coming

we are the weather and the world
we are the earth who receives
we are the seeds of the rain

poets waiting in a dry world

he draws back the curtains at dawn
the blackbird the dunnock the dove
sing whistle and flute
the tune of our thankfulness

Where is the Other World?

(for Pamela)

birdsong floods the ears
in early june
yellow bursts from buttercups and dandelions
greenness pours through every stick stem and blade
we dimly sense the other world
hidden in this world

in this world nothing helps the other world
we are bathed in television violence
trickery earnestness sickness despair confusion

we are tourists fleeing
the cruel concentration of shopping malls
bowing to the power of people in government
immensely stupid and cunning
we remember only the mind and the body

nothing is what it appears to be
in the weaving of the two worlds
we can not say it
we dimly sense it
at the entrance to the lily's throat
or waiting behind the irrefutable sun
or at the fatal traffic accident
or with the torturer washing his hands after work

everything in truth
gestures to that other world
shopping malls wars and fields of wheat
nothing is what it appears to be
your eye sees more than meets
the eye

Strimming into Green

heavy air holds everything in place
thunder growls like distant fighters

embroidered on the meadow opposite
bullocks black and white on green

greens hold sway
oak leaves dark beside beech like unripe fruit
alder and nettles hiding violet and viridian
a willow green-silver
longing to be an olive tree
leaves diffusing into pewter air

rain starts to fall, arriving briskly, rapping on the shed roof
like a well intentioned visitor, a midwife or a christian sect

i feel so sad
so sad a dog-rose hurts my heart
long to be a man of wisdom
soaring on the wings of love

all afternoon i spent
strimming into green: grasses thistles docks
in amongst them foxgloves campion buttercups
red admirals painted ladies
the spinning blade levelled small worlds
collateral insects scattered in panic

the bees from my hives began
to dive bomb me.
three times i was stung
i shut the strimmer down
expiating sad and angry feelings
right before a thunder storm
is not green thinking

my heart closes like a miser's fist
i sit here in the doorway of the garden shed
waiting for the storm to pass
a willow wanting to become
an olive tree

WAY TO TOP

Curriculum Vitae

rashid sits at the pc screen
making up true stories
pressing dimpled squares
to build a mock-up of his life

i didn't choose the bullish banker
and his rigid wife
i choose them now
parents who would
give me passage
through a world
playing at world war
as i did in my sun-bright sandpit
where everything was never-ending
exploration
mysterious exciting

school made a sad man
of a happy boy
put metal in my spine
stale air in my heart
in an interview i told dad
when i grow up
i want to be an artist or a farmer or a teacher
and he stood up mortified
expelled me from his study
he didn't know i'd seen
another kind of world
while falling from a cedar tree
bless his heart
he wanted what he wanted for me
a stuffed shirt rigid wife and two fat kids
worth of happiness

/the long...

the long-legged beauty
who i longed to love
but failed and failed again
she and i produced at last
two lovely daughters
i had to let the whole lot go
their trust my hopes
the metal in the spine
and the stale air too
what a teaching that was
it's more painful losing illusions
than losing health or wealth
only then
only then
can freedom grow
bless her heart too

two beautiful sons came next
by a woman i could love and trust
one day aged thirty seven i noticed i was
an artist and a farmer and a teacher
next day a petrol tanker
skidding on a snowy road
showed me my death
I haven't lived I haven't lived
screamed my dumb heart
the way opened
we set out in search of
the other kind of world

there's always more to lose
layers and layers of onion skins
a meeting with my master
changed the game forever
he took from me that
which i did not have
art mister nice guy and financial complacency
gave me what i had already
mystery excitement

/the other world....

the other world sends frequent invitations
with sweet companions i travelled through
its gently rounded hills and valleys
by wooded streams and
rivers full of leaping salmon
and too we lived
starvation homelessness
envy and rejection

sometimes the inspiration
of an unknown benefactor
lifted me
raised me for an infinite radiant moment
into an upper air of clarity and peace
the moment passed
gravity the world and the past asserted
their million-year-old rights
again i had to clear my overdraft
argue with an angry motorist
get sick greet death
devoid of spirit most of the time

mum and i met in her death
dad i never mourned
colonel and banker
are two categories of man
difficult to invite
into my heart
so now is a good time to welcome him
into the spacious
gently rounded landscape
of my love

i look back on my life's curriculum
(the word means race course from the root *to run*)
there was no track there is no record
just the circle of infinity
i heard my master say
the only journey is from here to here

i watch the ebb tide take its
pulpy flotsam to the sea
leaving
a small boy
playing in the sun-bright sand
where everything is never-ending
exciting and mysterious
pressing dimpled squares
tapping into life
a mock-up of a life

Toothache

A man barged into my bedroom. I had an abscess under my lower right canine tooth. The man was huge with branches growing from his head. And mottled green fatigue-type clothing. He said I have some words you need to take to heart. He threw a pile of them onto my bed and was gone.
What was that? Some sort of psychosomatic therapy? My girl friend was out shopping. I was far too taken aback to follow him.
I laid the words out on my sheet.
12 verbs, 3 adjectives, half a dozen adverbs and conjunctions and some nouns and prepositions. I lined them up in categories. The verbs were - **being** (twice) **do** (twice) **doings fill grows is is rooted suffers understand**. The adjectives - **different ineluctable mysterious**. The nouns were interesting; **earth emptiness present** (or it could be a verb) **tree**. The rest were commonplace parts of speech - **not any altogether however the** (twice) **what as from in to**.

I'm not a one for crosswords, scrabble or anything to strain the brain. Least of all while feverish. I tried a few sentences. The best that I could come up with was; **- do you present your fill as being ineluctable? - however what you understand is altogether different - the tree in the earth suffers mysterious rooted emptiness -**
then I got left with **being to any doings - grows from do is not**

What the fuck? It had a certain rough-hewn significance. I tried to get the words to form more sentences. I dozed.

The mystery man returned, bending his mighty head through the door. He said we need poetry to help us through both the tough and the tender phases of life. Then he said that poetry is not to express ourselves but to realise ourselves. I liked that. He laid the words out on my duvet. He made a gesture at me, maybe rude, maybe a warning, and once more he disappeared. I looked at the words. They were strangely affecting.

what you do
you do not understand

the earth suffers
from your doings

being is
however

altogether different
mysterious ineluctable

being is rooted
in the present

as any tree growing to fill
emptiness

Forms of Love

everything is love isn't it?

at night
half memories
flit like privet moths
against the dark pane
of the bedroom window

the mountain straight ahead
above the snaking road
the mountain somewhere in my Self
fading to infinity
the verges and the hedges
waving like Sargasso weeds
around the blunt end of the speeding car
the food we eat
all these things are forms of love
how could it be otherwise?

what about raw sex and filthy art
polluted air and income tax
and ticks and war
and TV spreading germs
the thousand million sperm that never find the egg
and angry letters to the editor?

I easily forget
they too are love
how could it be otherwise?

maybe I don't explain myself too well
that's love too
senseless

RASHID
II '97

Your Temple

If you ask me

to build you a place
of worship
a meeting place of sacred
and mundane
I will set up pillars made of
bone
suspend the floor above a
chasm
the roof will be a thatch of
sky
inside will be the endless emptiness of
You

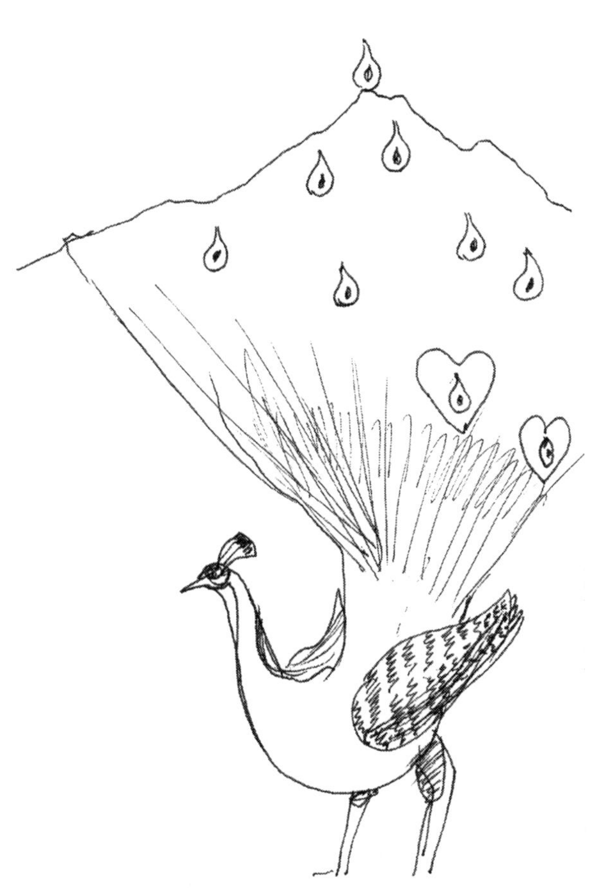

Both This and That

I wonder whether the steam of this bristling shower
Would be such a brilliant event
Were it not that I'd spent so many hours
In draughty, broken-down apartments.
And would this damp autumnal day
Offer up its mists so infinitely sweetly
Had I not lived where rivers cake and crumble in decay
Crying in the heat?

Stepping darkly from the razed house of divorce
I once had to walk the desert's loneliness
So that now I can walk on my own with friends
And delight in this journey without destination.
I have made risk and loss my hobbies
In order to sit at peace on the cushioned moss
Beneath the golden trees fragmenting
In their patterned bliss.

It seems to me that if we want to live in light
We have to wander in dark valleys
The meaning of our life is incomplete
Until both ends of the circle meet

Bad News Good News

drunk
on the divine
is what i want to be
when I grow up
i want to be a sufi poet
singing love songs to the ultimate reality grace
as we
about to crest
in glorious love
at full moon
in a perfumed bower
disappear become absent
or failing that
write a poem about bees
who
like some mythic creature
creature of imagination
know exactly where you're at
better than you know yourself
(are you present?
are you present to these bustling characters?)
tell how on summer afternoons i draw the flocked frame
up to eye level
ten thousand wings vibrate to cool the brood
solid form and also
formless
they take to the air
a ceaseless dance of electrons
scent of all the sweetness of the world
their humming sound turns gravity to grace
they are one and many
a mind both here
and elsewhere simultaneously

the bad news is i am grown up already
the good news is that we can close our eyes
and glide plummet
into the great rivering emptiness
in which everything
already
is

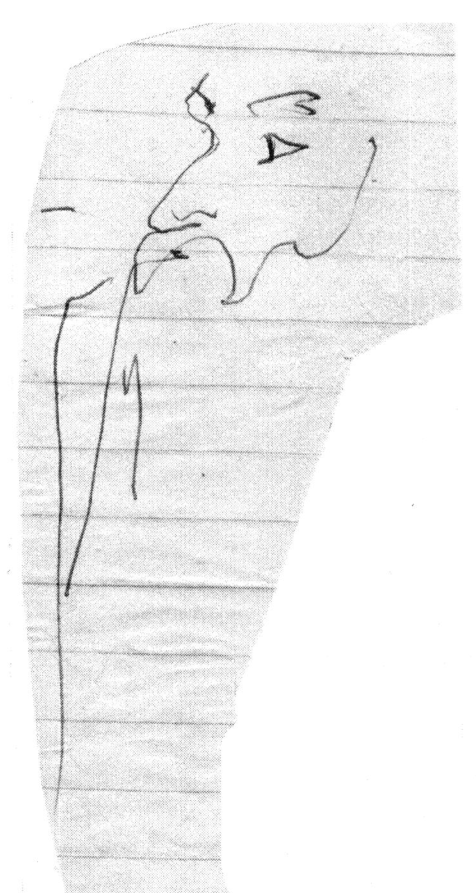

An Osho Leela Love Story

Half way through my stay at Osho Leela music festival my girl friend called to check if I had found another girlfriend

On that opening Tuesday afternoon I first noticed you
with the palest sky eyes ever

then on Wednesday morning I felt your
gold tanned calf

later I saw your fingerprint
in the curved lines of the mown hay

on Thursday you were there again
flirty in the haystack
with a body like a bouncy castle

Friday afternoon I heard you singing near my tent
in concert with recurring calls of doves

your sigh is like the grey wind in the poplars

before dawn on Saturday the brilliant
dew-drops

like the vanishing stars
represented you

and later in the long hug
that we had at coffee break I became aware of your power

on Sunday when you tapped me on the shoulder
showed me leaves laid out on the ground

in a pattern of mysterious significance
I suddenly recognised who you are.

Yes I'm talking to you - Joy - Love - Great Self - whatever you like to
call yourself!

Calling Names

worked in the orchard
cold
enough to freeze
your bollocks into brass
pollarded an ash pruned the old
apple
cut a laundry pole

got to thinking how we
can't
stop killing off
the earth how the hell
can anyone however well informed
begin
to understand the whole

made a mental list of
names
we call out in the
dark all of them
fearful and childish ideas
toy bears
just to console

Allah, Almighty, the Creator, Everlasting Father, God, The Gods, Jehovah, Lord of Lords, Our Maker, Ram, Supreme Being, Yahweh, etc.

who is this person who doesn't exist?
why does his worship seem to persist?
get lost! I tell him you holier-than-thou
i would - he says - but i don't know how.

/dusk falling...

dusk falling golden
willows
by the stream owl
in the woods above
everywhere we sense a hidden world
hidden
right inside the visible machine

absolute reality, all-that-is, first cause, the ground of all being, i am, oneness, presence, pure awareness, self, source, supreme energy, that, ultimate reality, universal consciousness, the void etc.

i live a simple life
watch
whatever happens
as if in a film
without any preference or beliefs i
enjoy
the passing scene

The Camera Man

Look at the camera please!
Try not to squint or frown
When I raise my hand I want you to freeze.
Don't look up or down

You're out of my control
Please don't take offence
What's that? I'm taking a bit of your soul?
Superstitious nonsense!

The man with the camera squats
Among the rush hour workers
His wives are posed for their tourist shots
Wearing their full length Burkhas

in the country of the Void

three amazed grandchildren
and i watch the enormous

futile leap of salmon
below the weir at Eggesford

later we examine acorns
for their little yellow tail-shoots

that root beneath the seething
leaf-mould in the oak copse near our house

we children of the earth are such clever fools
that our grandchildren may not inherit
a planet fit for human life
our great endeavour with our tools
is to eliminate one species every minute

waves of light weave a version of the moon
across the glossy void onto our retina
which then transmits them to our brain.
mind itself is like a delicate confection
spun from ice and sugar

my teacher friend says that in truth we're formless
so mind looks out at the vast emptiness
it feels we will disappear
unless it keeps on thinking thinking thinking . . . .

it has forgotten the deep relaxation of nothingness
her own teacher said that those who say
i must leave this world a better place for my children
are dreamers the world will never be better or worse.

the world is a dream of existence
like this one day like that another

you are not the world
awaken to that fact

yet we still prefer to spin out our
candyfloss lives when we need to listen

to the silence of the rivers and the woods
leap like trusting salmon into nothingness

live quietly in the house called Open Hearted
in a street called Open Handed

in a village whose name is Rest
in the country of the Void

All Ten Thousand Words

the blue sky is not blue
words are not themselves

the black glide of a jackdaw
through the boundary of vision

the journey that the butter knife is taking
while we talk of metaphors

thrush-song winding through the evening
like gold thread in a tapestry

sensations on the edges of our sense
are always closer to what is

to what is unseen right in front of us
beneath the inklings of this page

inside the dried up winter grass
driving through the purple storm above

words are not themselves
or what we talk about

poems bridge two worlds
the grain of sand and what

exists
in all ten thousand words

It Only Takes One To Tango

the house tonight is silent
humming
you could say the silence is alive

i do not want this poem written
when in pain i call out to you
i call out to you ma
but i'm already old and you are dead

my favourite anaesthetic is to fall in love
the gates of heaven open to strange eyes
i put off questions that i cannot ask
until the honeymoon is over

then i fix up with another
blame my mother
drink the milk i never drank
dance tangos
in the bright-lit cities of the night

the kind house creaks in the morning air
feeds me words i do not know
low clouds drink the dawn
a blackbird sings on a redbrick chimney

you could say that the living silence
has overflowed
satisfied me at its breast

it only takes one to tango

Haiku

Walking round sacred Mount Arunachala
This time
Hey! No poem!

What is this anger for my father?
Swifts circle the blue sky
I am he

An upright bicycle
A woven nylon bag
How many lifetimes?

I'm not at home in the new place
The old tenant keeps coming back
Today I found him in my bed

Haiku

Mind is a raging dog
Pulling at the worn leash
What if I let it go?

This sunny day I'm feeling peaceful
Which goes to show
I'm not at peace

Raindrops patter
On the oak leaves in my heart
In the tree trunks my lungs breathe

Winter sun on lily leaves
Come play in the forest
Of the lily

Bumper Stickers

Everything I've ever said's a lie
Today is different ~
I don't say anything!

beelight

winter solstice

a grey sun
long distanced from last summer's
green orgasm
from beaming green woods
saturating birdsong yellow rattle
and foxgloves flaming out across the nubile fields
then too the honey bees were orgasmic
on gleaming combs of nectar
contented humming rising from
a hundred thousand wings

now on the earth's winter ellipse
at the point of noon
cold vibrating air
fills with beelight

a moment of golden sweetness
always now
a lifelong moment

We are Well Protected

we are well protected
the coastline bristles with defences
land to air land to sea
air to air and all the waters mined

we crisscross to and from appointments
denounce traitors
interrogate suspicious persons
talk dirty to our neighbour's wife

let's keep our nose to the grindstone
until the big one comes
an accident
a scandal in the public body

an act of criminal intent
some wave beyond tsunami
everything we set up
obliterated

in the abandoned fortress
of the mind - if we're lucky
new views open up
silence grows like old man's beard

row on faded row of breakers
stretching to the line of tender sky
we have reached the visible frontier
of the other world

right here in this world
if you want peace
welcome disaster our greatest ally
hope for what disturbs the mind

The Real Poem

the real poem is without words
a cyclone
rising from an empty page

all day i was busy
transferring data to my laptop
finishing a trellis for the grapevine
opening my beehives to check for parasites
listening to the radio for election results

when my aunt passed away
she stopped clearing out her cupboards
she lay back
in the centre of the hurricane
i saw her leave

sitting silently at dusk
i listen to what can't be said
a shifting cloud of twenty million starlings
in a curving time and space
a nightingale's song in thunder
defying gravity

or sometimes i'm a soldier in a city under siege
making nightly sallies
through the gate of silence
into other peoples dreams
when all the time
all the time within the walls
sweet-water wells are plentiful

real poems have no words
whirlwinds
rising from an empty page

The Day of the Fox

Somewhere on the white page of this morning,
behind the digital alarm calls and the creaking floors,
windows framed with silver scales of moisture
smells of coffee and the hacking cough next door,
a poem lies in wait.

Today's the start of winter, All Souls Day;
sun moulds the trunks of oak with gold,
our neighbour's meadow, ever more
encircled by brigades of gorse and brambles,
glows blue and ochre
with the first frost of the year.

Unexpectedly, a fox trots past the window.
Foxes are my secret guides, they tell me things
I do not know I know
I call the missus but already he
is lost in motley shadow.
His faint calligraphy across the frost
spells out a coded message to his clan.

All Souls, it says is really one big Soul
like Allspice is one fragrant spice.
Imagine Allsoul is the energy that animates,
abides in woods and birds and rivers,
babies manifesting into women,
our beautiful round planet rolling patiently
around its burning star.

This Allsoul day the fox points to the soul,
reminds us it pervades the whole

The Other Country

We've always lived here in the border towns
As long as anyone remembers
We hang out in the markets and the bars
Watching sport and news and John Wayne movies

Only sometimes do we cross the border
As tourists to the country where the air
Is clear where rivers aren't polluted
And the people are both generous and free

We know that we can go and live there
In that spacious land It's just
That we prefer the dramas and
The updates on the war on terror

You know how you can win the war on terror?
Someone asked us over there Stop fearing it
Live here where life and death are allies
A coalition of the unavoidable

You know what? maybe i will emigrate
They say it's very easy
More like simple click and drag than relocation
Not so much a going but a coming

Maybe next week

Temporary Trees

"These old oak and beech trees were not kept for their timber or their beauty - they were left standing when the developers cleared the site building."

Sitting in their shade
In the great bowl of their silence
They close down all my striving
Shoulds and oughts
And can'ts

In their airy skill and earthy hug
They make a field
Impersonal ubiquitous
In which the life I
Think I ought to live
Evaporates

Oaks, blue tits, a grey squirrel
And this earnest writer fellow
We're all more or less useful
More or less beautiful
And only passing through
This temporary wood

This is our World

you're far too positive about everything he said
it's unbalanced
not real

the school of amnesia had taught her
to stay in her tight fitting boots
expect to be brought down a peg or two
learn to toe the line

in the silence they could sense the hiss
of her slow puncture

look out there she said at last
pointing to
a cloudless summer sky
the scent of hay in every breath
foxgloves in
their drooping purple congregation

listen to the radio she said
a man emerging from the underground
blood dripping from his head
horror in his eyes
face and clothes covered with the black confetti
of two beliefs divorcing

look at me
take my hand
feel my pleasure and my pain she said
this is our world
this is the world

the grasshoppers chirring on the lawn
are picked off by the thrush at dawn

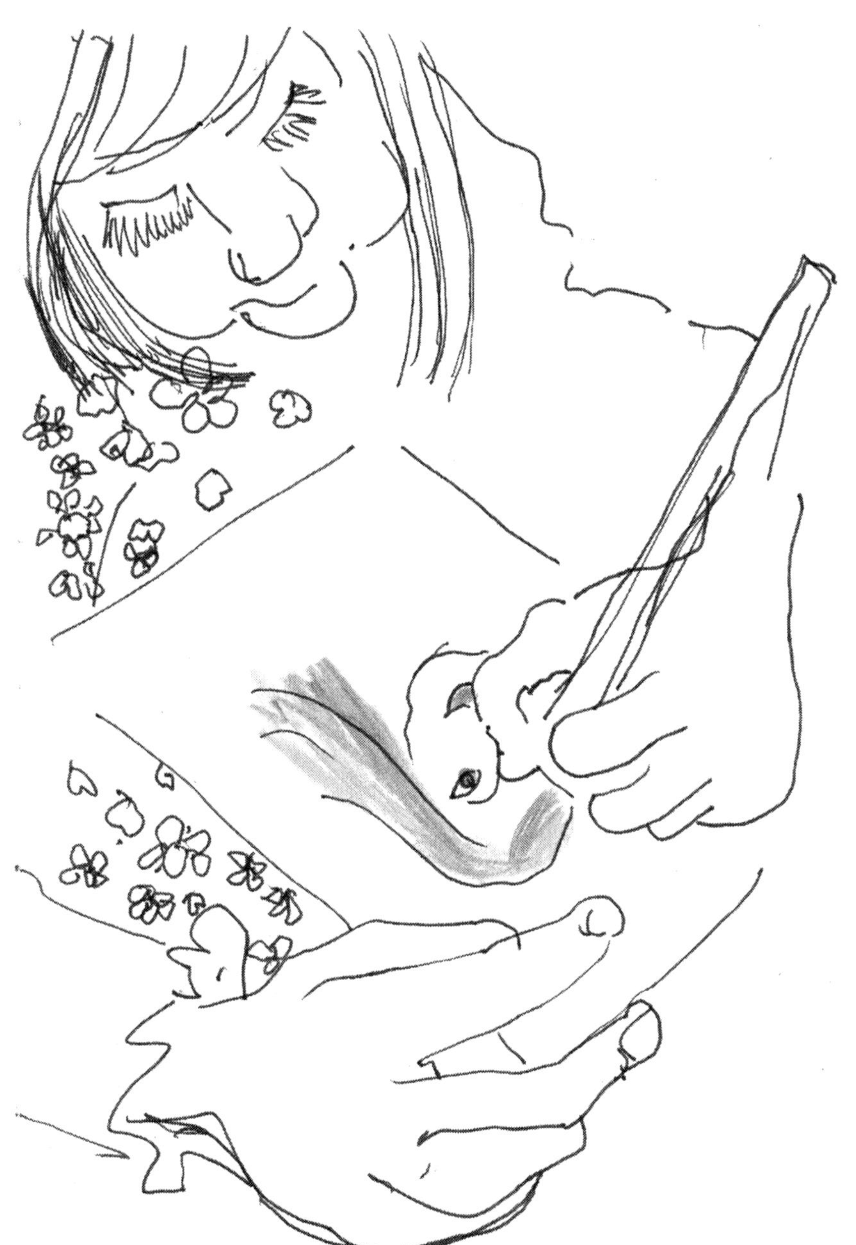

In the Forest of the Heart

in the virgin forest
of the heart
a call rings clear
as a chaffinches's song
'be still and know'

when an old giant
crashes
to the forest floor
creepers are the first away
striving for the light

i watched them on tv last night
blind tendrils
waving in their time-lapsed world
groping
using everything

to gain a purchase
stifle competition
he called them
opportunists
like us humans

in the forest of the heart
be still and know
means
do nothing
be nobody

the trees of the forest
rise and fall
make food for monkeys
become food for termites

knowing
rises in the heart
not knowing
guides our feet

www.ingramcontent.com/pod-product-compliance
Ingram Content Group UK Ltd.
Pitfield, Milton Keynes, MK11 3LW, UK
UKHW021332070726
13610UKWH00011B/33